The Power of Determination

By

Blessed Thabang Mobosi

The Power of Determination

Published by

William Jenkins
2503 4288 Grange Street
Burnaby BC V5H 1P2
Canada

williamhenryjenkins@gmail.com

http://williamjenkins.ca

Cell: 1-778-953-6139

ISBN: 978-1-928164-18-0

Dedication

I dedicate this book to my creator the almighty God. Thanks for the Solomonic wisdom and knowledge from above.

The Power of Determination

Author
Blessed Thabang Mobosi

I was born on 17 December 1997. I live in South Africa with my parents, with two young brothers and one sister.

I believe that my calling is to become a Financial Manager. I hope to study Commerce and Finance in university and specialize in Financial Management as a career. As well, I want to be an International Evangelist. My role model is Dag Heward Mills.

I am currently the Chairperson of the Student Christian Organization of Ritavi Circuit. I have about 26 schools under my leadership.

When I was eleven, I started to preach and motivate students at primary level at Ritavi Primary School located here in Nkowankowa, Limpopo.

I wish to reach out to the world with my motivational sermons, poems and speeches. I have been invited on many different occasions to act as minister. You can catch me at:

Email: Blessed.btm@gmail.com
Contact: +27 61 953 9726 or
         +27 78 506 5555

Acknowledgements

My thanks to Pastor Mr. & Mrs. C.A Emmanuel for your attributes upon my life; and to my wonderful teachers at Hudson Ntsanwisi senior secondary school, friends and mentees.

My thanks to Mr. William Jenkins, my publisher from Canada.

Thanks for the great acceptance of my first book "Destiny is a Matter of Choice"

To my wonderful parents Mr Antony Mobosi & Rosina Mothopane Mobosi, my father and mother. Thanks for your support.

The Power of Determination (Will Power)
By
Blessed Thabang Mobosi

The Power Of Determination

The Power Of Determination

Contents

The Power Of Determination

The Power Of Determination

The Power Of Determination

The Power Of Determination

The Power Of Determination

The Power of Determination

Introduction

In my perspective, determination is the ability to work hard to achieve an objective or the ability to establish a goal no matter how difficult it is to achieve. It is the most important thing that every one of us must bear in life.

Without determination, it is difficult to attain most of our life's objectives. When we are determined, we have a strong will, we are courageous and willing to give ourselves unto achievement and that's how the power of determination helps us. I define it as will power, the power of your willingness.

When people are determined, they have the willingness to drive or pass through difficulties; they push themselves to do things in their maximum best level. Determination is one of the powerful weapons that one can use to impact life.

You have To Be Determined If You are To Achieve.

Dreams and goals in life are established when you're determined about them. Being determined aims you working hard to achieve them, and also makes you work at your level best. You cannot unleash your full potential unless you have the will or the desire to do your very best at all times, and the willingness to work hard in doing your best at all times while passing through many of life difficulties that will come along your path of life.

Being determined gives you the strength and the ability to push yourself to do something; even if you're not willing to do it.

Examine All Great People In Life

All great achievers in life have made it to where they are today due to attainment to hard work, commitment and determination. You cannot just wake up in the morning and accomplish life's most

The Power Of Determination

difficult task, but with determination you can you wake up and decide to work it out.

How Determination Empowers You

It keeps us firmly concentrated on our chosen purposes. It is the tool that we use to keep defeat and failure far away from us from becoming permanent. Determination is something that can help your life become successful; without it you don't have the ability to achieve great things or better.

Your life is yours to control and to create whatever you want. In doing so, it takes determination to open a door of great achievement and overall happiness in your life. As well, determination makes us pursue a goal with energy and focus.

How To Keep Yourself Determined

Here are some things that you can do to keep yourself determined along the journey of life as you work towards fulfilling your goals and destiny.

- Seek counsel
- Have faith and hope
- Be discipline and determined
- Remember your goals and purpose
- Know what you want
- Be optimistic
- Be prioritized
- Avoid laziness
- Be willing to pay the price
- Know what the price is
- Avoid discouragement
- Seek for a solution when there is a problem
- Believe in yourself
- Don't be afraid of failure
- Oppose adversity
- Don't procrastinate

The Power Of Determination

- Be willing to do more
- Overcome fear and doubts
- Don't be satisfied
- Make things happen
- Don't give up on yourself

Seek Counsel

Plans go wrong for lack of advice; many advisers bring success. *Proverbs 15:22s*- (NLT)

Sometimes we come through different situations that make us weary, weak or discouraged and even confused. When we seek counsel, it helps us to overcome that negative mind; it injects us with the empowerment to arm ourselves with strength and determination.

Have faith and hope

Now faith is being sure we will get what we hope for. It is being sure of what we cannot see.-*Hebrew11:1-* (NLV)

Our life is lived by faith. We do not live by what we see in front of us.-*II Corithians 5:7*-(NLV)

As a person you must have faith. Having faith gives you the strength and ability to overcome fear and doubt. It also makes you believe in yourself; striving in your heart to hope for more without giving up. For faith is your goal; it is the root of your determination.

The challenges you face and what you come across must not stop you from reaching your objectives or from moving forward. Instead of looking at what you come across in terms of difficulties, you must look ahead of those hurdles and continue with your journey, thinking about glory ahead.

The Power Of Determination

Be Disciplined And Maintain Self Control

Without discipline and self-control it is difficult to stick to the path of taking action and pursue it to the end. If you've got to make it to the end, you must be disciplined and be able to control yourself to maintain some of life's rules of success, such as avoiding procrastination, being able to work hard and sacrifice. Therefore upon any step of achievement, be disciplined and maintain self-control.

Remember Your Goals And Purpose

You can also strengthen your self-determination by remembering your goals and purpose and telling yourself you'll endure to the end until your will is established. This will help you to be determined to endure pain and suffering without having them stop you from reaching your destination and also help you to strengthen yourself when events are in your favor. As the bible says in Romans chapter eight verse 28 that "And we know that all things work together for good to those who love God, to those who are the called according to His purpose."

Remember your purpose and goals, always having faith, while thinking of the glory ahead, and do not give up. One example of a person who did not give up until he fulfilled his purpose is my master Jesus. Look unto his life as a good example of endurance with determination:

Let us keep looking to Jesus. Our faith comes from him and he is the one who makes it perfect. **He did not give up when He had to suffer shame and die on a cross. He knew of the joy that would be His later. Now He is sitting at the right side of God.**-*Hebrews 12:2* -(NLV)

Know what you want

If there is one gift that you can give yourself in life, it is to be what you want. Always remind yourself who you are, where you come from and where you're going. This will keep you courageous and determined always to move forward to the next step. It is the

4

The Power Of Determination

power of determination and without it you're just passing by in the start of your life. One thing that makes a difference among a follower, a winner, a loser and a leader is the power of determination. Without it you can plan, but you'll not accomplish much in life.

Remember winners never quit and quitters never win. Winners never quit because they are determined not to quit. Losers never try. You'll never know you'll make it if you don't try. Always remember winners never quit and quitters never win.

If you have determination, nothing can stop you from completing a particular course of action to achieve your goals or to bring your dreams into reality. One of the greatest weapons you can have in your life is the weapon of determination. If you have it, you'll have everything you hope for in life. You're where you are in terms of being successful or unsuccessful due to the level of determination and commitment to your goals.

Be Optimistic
Surely there is a future, and your hope will not be cut off.- *Proverbs 23:18(ESV)*

Optimistic, according to the Cambridge Advanced Leaners dictionary is defined as "hopefully believing that good things will happen in the future". A determined person must be generally optimistic and know what he or she wants to achieve. Knowing what you want helps you to plan and work out how you'll get to your destination, just as being able to look past a shadow to see light so that you can get to where you want to be.

Someone who lacks determination will not have the mindset to look for a bright side in things and will be settled with whatever he or she has. Being optimistic plays a big role in your improvement in allowing you to know you can do better and actually doing it, which is the key to determination.

The Power Of Determination

Be Prioritized

There is a special time for everything. There is a time for everything that happens under the heaven. *Ecclesiastes 3:1*(NLV)

A person who is determined to achieve any task of priority must be able to plan and act according to time and go from one major important goal to the next. Priorities are necessary for a determined person. You must know the relative importance of everything you're doing all the time. Prioritizing your life helps you to keep your goals in check due to time and also makes it easier for you to accomplish them.

Avoid Laziness.

A person who is determined to be successful in life must by all means fight against laziness and must be willing to work hard.

Being lazy makes one go into a deep sleep, and a lazy man will suffer from being hungry. *Proverbs19:15*(NLV)

If you're not determined to fulfill your own dream, you will be fulfilling somebody else's dream.

The hand of those who do their best will rule, but the lazy hand will be made to work. *Proverbs 12:24*(NLV)

If you're not determined to fight against laziness, you're not likely to make it in life. People who are lazy end up becoming products of poverty.

The soul of the lazy person has strong desires but gets nothing, but the soul of the one who does his best gets more than he needs. *Proverbs 13:4*(NLV)

If you don't fight laziness, by allowing it into your life will cause you poverty.

He who works with a lazy hand is poor, but the hand of the hard worker brings riches. *Proverbs 10:4*(NLV)

6

The Power Of Determination

Work hard and you'll be rich. Overcoming laziness and fighting through to achieve your objectives will be of great worth to you.

The lazy man will not cook the food he has caught, but the man who does his best has what is of great worth. Proverbs 12:27.
(NLV)

The lazy man buries his hand in the dish, and will not even bring it to his mouth again. *Proverbs 19:24*(NLV)

Do you want to rule? To rule means to be in charge. It takes determination to work hard. Only those who work hard will be in charge. If you don't work hard and allow laziness to be your master, someone who works harder than you work will be in charge of you.

You'll totally become a slave. You'll be forced into hard labor. You'll find yourself in hands of people and places where you never wanted or wished to be. You won't be fulfilling your dream by then. You'll be working to help others fulfill their dreams.

Be Willing To Pay The Price of Endurance
You know that only one person gets a crown for being in a race even if many people run. *I Corithians 9:24* (NLV)

During your journey to great success, you will encounter hardships and challenges. There will be times when you will want to quit or feel like quitting and giving up and going back to doing something else. The quality that guarantees your success is the willingness to stick, to battle with anything until your dream comes true. That's the power of determination.

Achieving dreams usually requires some level of sacrifice. It might require you to put something aside in favor of working towards your dreams, investing all your time in your dreams and objectives, even saving or giving up a few hours of sleep each night.

Being lazy makes one go into a deep sleep, and a lazy man will suffer from being hungry. *Proverbs 19:15*(NLV)

7

The Power Of Determination

Many people proclaim a desire to achieve their goals, yet they are unwilling to pay the price it takes to make their dream a reality. You can't have a reward unless you have paid the price. There is nothing for free in this planet called earth. Anything that is free to you means that someone else has paid for it.

Know What the Price Is

If you don't know what is truly required to make your dreams a reality, investigate what it will take to achieve your desired result. Research the cost other people had to pay to achieve the dreams; especially those with similar dream or purpose to yours. You can go to the internet to do research about other successful people in whom you're interested. You can find out how they made it to where they are today. You can also read their books to gain their kind of experience. You can pay a visit to those who are nearby to interview them.

Then, if the price is something that you're willing to pay, commit yourself to achieving your dream, no matter what it takes. The determination to do what is required of you is the perseverance that will help you to face all the challenges, setbacks, pains, hurts and wounds thus finally coming out with victory.

Avoid Discouragement

No matter how well you plan and how well you execute your plans, you are going to come across all the enemies of determination such as setback and failure along your way to your ultimate triumph. Sometimes the world will test your commitment to the goal you're pursuing by challenging your determination.

Adversity is a great teacher. It gives you the opportunity to develop abilities and makes you to learn new lessons, develop new part of yourself and makes you take right decision with caution.

Seek a Solution When There Is a Problem

Problems, challenges and hardships of life are some of the things that will wrestle with your power of determination. To avoid losing

The Power Of Determination

focus and courage, seek guidance or solutions from mentors or anyone who can help in that state. This will help you to hold on to your determination. The longer you're determined, the greater the chance that you'll win your battle no matter how hard it seems. The longer you persist, the more you're likely to be successful in life.

Believe In Yourself

Being successful in life is all about having belief in yourself, truly believing that you're something unique, something special, with a great value. You know God has made us unique. We were wonderfully and fearfully made by him.

If you believe that you're one of the best actors, singers, musicians, dancers, motivators or teachers in the world, you'll be totally different. That is, if you're totally sure of who you are and if you do believe in yourself. If you don't believe in yourself, your dreams and goals will never be a reality. You have to believe in yourself. You can do it.

Everyone has a mental doubt in life as a conflict in the mind. Even the most successful people who we admire have doubts, but they don't stay there. You have to untie your hand from negative thoughts in every moment and overcome them with positive action. It takes will power within yourself to handle the situation in that moment.

Believe in yourself and change your mentality. One of the speakers that masquerades as Zig Ziglar states that "If you want to change your world, first control what goes into your mind".

Don't Be Afraid Of Failure

Failure is not an option, it's something that occurs when we try. It becomes a choice when we quit. When you try something, keep yourself determined to live as if failure does not exist. Indeed it does not. Who cares? It appears when we give in to choices such as quitting; but live as if it does not exist. It is just a label.

The Power Of Determination

Don't let anyone steal your dreams with negative comment. If they have failed, they have. You're not them. They are; you are. Tell yourself that you can do it. If others can do it, why not? Don't let them make failure optional to you. Do you want to be great in life, not first, not second, but great? Just be determined.

When someone tells you that, "you can't do something", tell them "You've got the wrong person. I will show you that I can do anything". Tell yourself you can do the impossible. Why not?

Jesus looked at them and said, "This cannot be done by men. But with God all things can be done." Matthew 19:26. 5 (NLV)

I can do all things because Christ gives me the strength. *Philippians 4:13* (NLV)

Oppose Adversity

I want you to think about your dreams and goals, the kind of a future you hope for. Don't let setbacks stop you from chasing your dreams. It is possible you can make your dream come to existence. Just keep on working day in and day out. Most people stop working on making their dreams a reality. They stop stretching themselves; they stop pushing themselves from achieving more after a certain objective has being accomplished.

They do only what they have to do, forgetting that doing the same thing will give you same result. They raise a family, earn a living and die. But people who work for their dreams to come true are not afraid of adversity. You have to be ready to fight anything that comes your way as an obstacle that could prevent you from moving ahead. You have to know that in your process to work for your dreams, you're going to incur a lot of disappointment, a lot of failure, a lot of pain, a lot of setbacks and a lot of defeat, but in the process of all these you'll discover something about yourself that you don't know about yourself now.

You'll realize that you're much more powerful than you imagined. Therefore for this purpose, align yourself with people who will

The Power Of Determination

encourage you, people who can empower you, people from whom you can learn, people with whom you'll grow. Look at your life, where you are and where you want to go. Don't worry about your age and uncertainty. You have to say yes to your life, yes to your dreams, yes to your gifts and talents, yes to your unfolding future and yes to your full potential. Why not? The future is unlimited right now. How do you want to walk it? How far do you want to go in life? No one knows where you're going. No one knows what you're capable of or what is possible for you. For we all have the power to change our choices, the power to change our lives and the power to explore our thoughts to decide where we want to go.

Don't Procrastinate

(Every time is a perfect time)

There will never be any point in your life that is the right time to do a great thing. If you're waiting for that perfect moment, the perfect moment is not going to come. You know that you must create that perfect opportunity, that perfect situation and that perfect time. Things don't just happen. Something has to be done in order for things to happen.

A lot of people become satisfied and comfortable; they never work hard enough to get the exact result. They just stop hanging on 'til they are victorious. They never allow the victor within them to manifest itself. People go to jobs they do not like even jobs that makes them sick. Realise that if you're not doing something that is fulfilling your dream, even if you're working, you're committing a spiritual suicide. Later you'll see people quitting and giving in to other things. When you check, most of them have nothing to show for their effort. Is that not procrastination?

When you have a goal that stretches you, a goal that takes you out of your comfort zone; you'll find some talents and abilities that are strange to you. This happens to people who are determined to take a step further to explore more about the hidden treasures of

11

The Power Of Determination

success. These people are willing to be more successful and willing to achieve more than they have already accomplished.

Be willing to do more

Every success is built on the ability to do better than "just enough". Unless you attempt to do something different from what you have already mastered you'll never grow. You'll never know what you can do unless you take a step to do it. If you're not where you want to be, if you don't have that which you wanted to have, if you're not where you should be by now, it shows that you're not making any sacrifice.

Be willing to do more. You must set a goal and work to make your dream a reality because if you don't, you're going to work for someone else to make their dream a reality.

Overcome Fear And Doubts

Fear is not real. The only place it can exist is in our thoughts. When we think about the future, we may be worried about what we do not see. These may be events that may not occur or things that do not exist. Where we are going is not according to the happenstance in the present nor in the future, but the choices we make will determine what we will achieve.

All in all, it is with determination. You have to overcome fear in such a way that all you can do is to step into your dream. The first step is to see yourself as a different person, a person who is led by self-determination, a person with self-determination. You can do it.

While you're not yet where you want to go, you can't be where you are now for the rest of your life. It doesn't matter what life looks like or what is happening now. Every day you wake up, you must have energy; you must have a passion to bring about a change. You have to think about what your life is and what your life will be without any course of any forward movement.

Fight against every fear that will make you abandon your dreams and all that you have to accomplish. Fight against the fear that will

The Power Of Determination

make you hide and the fear that will make you come up with all sorts of excuses. If you lose to this fear, you will end up not achieving your dreams.

There are people who say I tried once or twice and they use that as an excuse not to try again. Even if you have never made it, and even if you have experienced defeat and failure, those do not make you a failure. There is difference between failing and being a failure. If you didn't get the result that you aimed for, don't give up. Don't confuse who you are with the result that you produced. Do what you can, where you are, with what you have, but don't become satisfied; always strive for more.

Some people are afraid they will fail or even worse that they will actually succeed. As a result they don't bother to take the steps to achieve their objectives. Such people lack belief in themselves and their potential. They think that if they fail, everyone will have a negative thought about them. It is because of their mindset and the kind of nature in them that makes them not take a step forward. Realize that you can achieve anything you set your mind to when you focus. Believe in yourself and your abilities and others will too. After all, to fail does not mean you're a failure. You become a failure only when you stop trying.

The fact that you are still on the battleground proves that you're not a failure. Don't let fear rule over you. Fear robs you of your true potential because it is the parasite that feeds on you the host. When fear comes into your mind, heart and upon all your being, resist it with immediate effect.

What is the benefit of allowing fear to turn you back? What is the benefit of giving up on you? What is the benefit of not stepping on life and taking life on? What is the benefit of that?

You have to ask yourself: "How long am I going to allow this to hold me back?" Take the best step now to come out of fear. Tell yourself that fear will not stop me. I didn't come this far to be

The Power Of Determination

stopped.

You have to believe in yourself and that one day your moment will come. "Impossible" is just a word. It's found only in the dictionary of fools. That is the only place where it is found.

Don't Be Satisfied

Always know that regardless of where you are now, you can enjoy more. Why don't you decide now that you can expand your world? People can learn anything. You can learn too if you work on your dreams. Show your critics many times that you aren't going to give up. The challenge is to hold on. I say that if you hold on to your dreams, the universe is on your side.

If you don't decide to move forward with your dreams; if you don't make a choice to live your life; if you don't take a step to say 'yes' to your life, you'll never live for yourself and you'll never work for yourself. In fact, you'll never be successful in life.

Your life is short and unpredictable. What do you say? There will always be tomorrow which is another day to try. You can't give up. I don't believe you came this far to stay where you are for the rest of your life. Tomorrow will always come and go. You still have much more to accomplish. Can you?

Why don't you take every choice of your life to establish more? Why not more? You can still expand your business, build more locations and grow your territory. Yes, you are worth the result. You're worth the effort. If you've got to pull something off to bring about a revolution take it off and life will never be the same again.

Be Determined To Make Things Happen.

If you don't develop the courage to fulfill your purpose and if you spend your time convincing other people to try to get their approval, you'll lose your determination. Other people will convince you that what you're doing at your level best doesn't have any value and you'll give up on your dreams. If we spend

The Power Of Determination

most of our life trying to find security and satisfaction, we will end up with most of our potential, gifts and talent in the grave.

In life, you are here today and gone tomorrow. The fact that you're still breathing means you have a lot of work to do and you owe it to yourself to do it. Look in the mirror and ask "Am I living my life the way I want to?" If you don't act on your dreams and if you don't take a step of determination, you'll never make things happen and you'll be left behind. Remember the best time is now while you're still zealous. Realize how great you could be and express yourself with determination and know that you can make things happen.

We all have twenty four hours a day, three hundred and sixty five days in a year, fifty-two weeks and 12 months. How many days have you lived on the earth? How much time do you have left? What else are you living for and what do you want to accomplish? What do you want us to remember you for when you're no more?

It is time for you to make things happen, You got to work on your mentality and self and tell yourself that you can do it. One idea with determination can change your life. As you convince yourself, you'll see changes begin to take place. Whatever you are, whatever you have and whatever you do, do it with all your strength.

Is there anything you want? You have to do whatever is necessary until you reach the best to the state of what is required for its occurrence.

The great gift that you can receive with determination is you growing stronger through the hardships and the challenges. Don't give up. Make things happen.

Don't Give Up On Yourself

Don't fall from the goals too quickly. Many people give up so easily. Don't give up in any step you take. Every stumbling block you come across may have only one way forward. You have to hang on and push forward. Tell yourself that you deserve victory and nothing will stop you. It doesn't matter what happened yesterday. We don't give up. We don't surrender to failure and defeat. We see differently and our rewards are different.

Place Determination at Work

It is true that ability is not as important as determination. Determination takes courage, willingness, ambition, inspiration and strength. People with any kind of ability, gift or talent should plan to put determination with it. Determination takes will power and effort. A person's ability will manifest only with determination.

I have the ability to write inspirational essays, yet sometimes I am too lazy to write. I am always determined to overcome laziness and work to bring my desires into reality. I have the gift to inspire people in different ways. Even though the gift is there, it takes determination to manifest the gift to its full potential in such a way that it can inspire to its maximum.

We can do anything we want, but it takes the unwavering power of determination to act on the conviction that we have. Willpower will help us to take action to bring to manifestation the goals we choose. We have the liberty to choose and decide the kind of life we want to pursue. With faith in God and confidence in ourselves, with a strong determination, we can achieve the impossible.

For God can do all things. *Luke 1:37* (NLV)

Realize the most difficult dreams and achieve excellence and incredible success in life. When you think of difficulty, ask yourself why can't I do it?

I can do all things because Christ gives me the strength. – *Philippians 4:13* (NLV)

Determination Brings Achievement

Every day I wonder where will I be when I get out of high school. What will life throw at me at that moment? Well I am determined

The Power Of Determination

to commit myself to my studies. I believe in myself and will definably reach my destination. What I need is more determination to do so. Determination is one of the things that keeps me going each day and helps me finish and complete all that is required of me each day.

Being determined gives me enough strength to become a graduate student. Determination is a wonderful thing. You do not need to give up because you know you can do it. Determination requires you being positive in all the aspects of your life, no matter what. You can have the ability to do it; but are you determined to make it happen? I know I can. Can you?

Self-Determination Leads To Prosperity

Determination is one of the greatest pillars of prosperity; without it we cannot reach our destination. I believe if you want to be prosperous you must be determined. If you're not, when you come through obstacles and hurdles such as difficulties of life or when something holds back or when you face discouragement, you'll quit and never pass the barrier.

Other people like me have the power to motivate you to try harder, but on the other hand you need to be the one to have determination by dedicating yourself to keep going and to continue fighting for your goal.

When I received my school result one day and found that I was not promoted to the next grade and had to repeat the class for a whole year due to the fact that I had not satisfied the requirement of two subjects out of seven, I was very discouraged and thought of changing my school to another school. Well, later on, I came back to my senses and told myself that am going back to the same school, same class and same subjects.

I couldn't accept that I am a failure. I overcame negative thought. As well, I am a well-known person and didn't consider what people would say about my having to repeat a grade. I was

The Power Of Determination

determined not to accept every bad comment and was ready to prove any critics wrong. I wouldn't allow bad comment and negative people to keep me from achieving my goals. I am glad to say that ever since then I've always being determined to pass to the next grade with quality marks. Soon I will be glad to say I am a high school graduate.

Many people in life influenced me to remain determined and to stay on the right path to accomplish my goals. I have always surrounded myself with positive people.

My mom and dad are all positive determined people. They have achieved great things in their lives. My father has his own household chemical production company and my mom has her own transportation business. They are both self-employed, determined and believe in themselves. They have always inspired me to believe in myself, my gifts talent and abilities and to hold onto my studies which are the solid foundation of success. As a result, I didn't want to disappoint the people who have supported me and believed in me. I would not be where I am today without the people who supported me and without my self-determination.

Prove them wrong via Determination

Beware of vision, dream and passion killers, family and friends in most cases. Family and friends in most cases could be the first that could talk you out of something that you're passionate about, excited about and that which you have. It can be a talent, ability or potential and even your dreams in most cases. Most people that have no dreams will wake up every day to try to talk you out of your own dream. They are people without a purpose and they don't have any ambition.

The most motivation I've ever received in my life is from people who told me that I couldn't do something. You know why? When they told me that I couldn't, I was bound and determined that I could. Tell me I can't do it and I will prove you wrong. I can, through Christ Jesus, who strengthens me. People will fight to slow

The Power Of Determination

you down, turn you around and cause you to move backward. If you let them do it, your determination is gone.

Tell yourself "I can". "I can" will do you one thing. It will keep you determined to get your mission accomplished. Who has the right to stop you from who you want to become in life and where you want to be? It is your right to make your own choice of where you want to go and be who you want to be.

So beware of people who are ungrateful. Do not let them stand in your way on your road to success. No matter how bad your day may be, they will bring you even lower. Think of the biggest discourager in your life. They are not really your discourager. You are. You don't think that you can. You can. Think about it; know that you can.

If you haven't done it yet, keep on striving, keep on walking. Don't quit until you reach your destination. Things don't come easily. You have to work for them. Do yourself a huge favor, keep yourself going; you might not make it now, but you will one day.

Use Your Gifts

Imagine you're standing around your grave. Standing with you are your unfulfilled potentials with the ghost of the ideas you didn't bring into action, the ghost of the talent you didn't use. You are standing there as a ghost, angry, displeased and disappointed in yourself. We are coming to you because you could have brought us unto life and now we had to follow you to the grave because you refused to manifest your abilities.

So, how many ghosts are going to be at your bedside when your life comes to an end? I am speaking about your gifts, talent and potentials that have not being used. Are they going to the grave with you?

In order to do something new you must be born again, by having a positive mentality. You have gifts, talents and potentials that you probably don't realise you have now. The first step is to live your

The Power Of Determination

calling and accept it. What is it that you have? Tell yourself what things that you can do. Make these happen.

On the other hand, you'll fail at some point in your life. If you accept it, you'll lose. You will be embarrassed sometimes. There is nothing wrong with that, but you have to stand up and strive for success with determination. You don't have to be anybody. Don't spend your life pretending to be someone else. Be yourself and don't be afraid of failure. It's being the original you that brings out your uniqueness, which is the first key to greatness.

Don't forget to believe in yourself, your gifts, talents and abilities. You have to trust in something, your life destiny. That will give you the confidence and the determination to follow your own path. You have some special stuff in you. There is a genius in you. There is a victor in you. You are born to win, born to reign in life. You are worth it and you have the power to achieve it.

Whatever you have, whatever your gift is, what are you going to do with what you have? We have to control our hours, our minutes and even seconds of every week, month and year. Don't wait until opportunities are closed or your abilities are no longer present. You may discover that you can't recover. Now it's not too late. You have that potential in you.

Remember you're always in control of your destiny. Go into action with your dreams and don't avoid the fights. Get into the places where the most fights are. Get knocked down so you can learn how to hold onto your decision.

Examples of people who were determined as reported in the Bible:

Esther

Esther was determined to set her people free from Haman's schemes to destroy the Jews. Mordecai, the uncle of the queen, had

The Power Of Determination

exposed the plans of Haman to kill the king so that he could take over the kingdom. For this very reason, Mordecai was a Jew and Haman promised to pay the king's storehouse to have the Jews destroyed, his reason being that Mordecai as a Jew had exposed his plans. Now, Esther the queen was also a Jew so Modecai had told Esther all that had happened and showed her the letter that was written to Susa to have all the Jews destroyed.

In those time they was a law that stated any woman or man who goes to the king's Royal palace room without being called, would be put to death unless the king holds out his special golden stick to him so that he may live. Therefore, Queen Esther remembered that she has not been called to come to the king for thirty days. Her uncle told her that, "who knows, whether God had placed her as a queen for this purpose". She came up with a plan to deliver her people.

After the fasting, she went to the king and she found favor in the sight of God and before the king, for the king had held up his golden stick, so that she should live. Then she asked for a request that Haman and the king must be at supper with her. During that supper, the queen made known unto the king all that troubles her heart. Haman's plans were exposed to the king. Esther found favor in the sight of the king. Haman was hanged and the Jew was liberated from his plans. The king remembered Mordecai and rewarded him for his loyalty.

Now if Esther was not determined to fulfill all the purposes, the Jews would have destroyed and we don't know what would have happened to her as a Jew, but she wouldn't find joy, peace and happiness as a queen after the destruction of her people. She was determined and paid the price with sacrifice of fasting for three days with no food and water while making her petition before God whom all the heart of kings are in his heart. Then God turned the heart of the king unto her direction through her determination to deliver her people as well in sacrificing.

The Power Of Determination

The Four Leprosy Men

The four Leprosy men were determined to move forward with their lives.

In this time in the lives of these men, they faced challenges of rejection, hunger and they were sick with leprosy disease. Remember in those days of the Old Testament if you had leprosy you had to be taken far away from the people to be alone.

He shall remain unclean all the days during which he has the infection; he is unclean. He shall live alone; his dwelling shall be outside the camp. *Leviticus13:46*(NASB)

Command the sons of Israel that they send away from the camp *every leper* and everyone having a discharge and everyone who is unclean because of a dead person. *Numbers5:2* (NASB)

Now the lepers were sent out of the city; they were now outside the city gate. The problem they had was not only that they had leprosy, in this time there was "famine in the land" meaning that they lacked food. Perhaps hunger struck them as part of their challenge. But one thing I love about these four men is that they took a positive decision with determination among themselves.

Now there were four leprous men at the entrance of the gate; and they said to one another, "Why do we sit here until we die? *II Kings 7:3* (NASB)

These men knew that if they just stayed at the gate entrance as rejected people, they would die of hunger. On the other hand, they knew if they returned to the city, they would be killed or stoned to death. They said if, "we stay here we will die and if we go back to the city they is no food there and the king still may give a command of our death. Therefore, let us die while moving forward. We will go to the Syrians camp".

22

The Power Of Determination

With this determination, I believe these men obtained favor in the sight of God because there was a war between the Syrians and the Israelites. While they were moving, the bible tells us in II Kings 7:5 that:

For the Lord had made the Syrian army to hear a sound of war-wagons and horses and army of many soldiers.

These sounds of war-wagons and horses and army of many soldiers was heard while these lepers were moving forward to the camp or tents of the Syrians. These lepers finally got to a place where they was enough food for them, and all that they needed to be comfortable. When the Syrians heard those sounds, they flew away and the lepers acquired their possessions. Afterwards, the lepers went to the city to report to the king for the food that the Syrians left behind was enough to feed the whole city. It was through the determination of the lepers that God saved the city from hunger.

Things That the Determined Don't Do

Remember all the successful people that we have in our world have activities that they keep constant to keep them going and they have some actions that they do not do.

The Determined Don't Give Up On Their Goals

Irrespective of how tough life is or how difficult things get, the determined do not give up on their dreams or any of their life objectives. For this purpose, you must have a powerful reason that keeps you going. If you want to be more determined, decide first that you will not give up until you achieve your goal. Get clarity on your reasons why you do that thing or why you must achieve it and what the consequence of failing will be. The better informed you are about the consequences of failing, the greater level of your determination will be. Most people who fail in their dream fail not from lack of ability, but from lack of commitment.

The Power Of Determination

The Determined Don't Let Failure Stop Them

The determined understand that they can fail initially and frequently but will succeed eventually. They are silent and this is why they often make greatest comebacks.

However, what many fail to do is to have flexibility. Hitting the wall with your head hoping that it will break is not determination. It is stupidity. Determined people will continue to try new things and keep changing their approach until they achieve their desired outcome. They are like a palm tree; they will bend in the blowing wind and will come back to their original position. Most people think that they themselves are determined when, in fact, they are not. Many even end up broken and battered.

The Determined Do Not Let Fear of Failure Stop Them.

Most people with a dream give up before they even start because of fear or the fear of what the outcome may be. They quit before they even start, but determined people are the opposite. For them not taking a step forward and not trying it is a burden that is too much to bear. Their fear of having to admit they did give it a try motivates them and keeps them moving forward.

If fear is stopping you, set an immediate, painful and probably a public consequence of not trying or starting. When you have a consequence for not giving it a try that is more painful than the fear of failure, you will tap into your determination with informed decisions knowing the consequences of not giving it a try. You will never know you cannot do something until you try it. Do it, then you will feel motivated to do it. If you don't start, it's certain that you won't finish.

The Determined Don't Let What They Don't Know Stop Them

They are willing to grow, ask lots of questions and fall on their face a few times until they achieve their outcomes.

The Power Of Determination

Understand that your current limitations in life are not permanent. Your present situation is based on how you spent your past. Start taking a new action today and you will create a new future. Determination is only fruitful if you are willing to take a step and grow further.

The Determined Don't Fear Rejection

They are willing to ask many people for advice until they get what they want. The greatest entrepreneurs, executives, sales people and good business men and woman are the ones who do not allow rejection to stop them. The reason is that their reason to succeed is greater than their fear.

Some People Who Were Once Rejected:

Albert Einstein

He did not speak until he was four and did not read until he was seven. He was subsequently expelled from school and was not admitted to Zurich polytechnic school. Long story short, he came around overcame rejection with determination to become great. He is one of the greatest physicists of the 20th century.

Oprah Winfrey

She was an evening news reporter and apparently got fired because she couldn't sever her emotions from her stories. Eventually, fired from the producer of Baltimore's WJZ-TV but with determination, she overcame rejection and took a step forward to bring a change in her life and to prove them wrong. Today she is a multi-millionaire influencing the world in a great way.

Bill Gates

Bill Gates didn't seem like a shoe-in for success after dropping out of Harvard and starting a failed first business called Traf-O-Data. While this early idea did not work, with determination Bill Gates with co-founder Paul Allen created the global empire that is Microsoft. Today he is the richest man in the world.

The Power Of Determination

The list of successful people who had to use determination to overcome rejection is endless. You can find more examples on the internet. If you want to achieve something significant, you are going to be rejected. To overcome it, be determined about moving forward.

One Story of Rejection from the Bible - Joseph.

Joseph had a dream whereby he saw the sun, the moon and twelve stars bowing before him. Interpreting the dream, it was his mother and father bowing before him. Joseph was hated by his brothers. They rejected him and he did not find a place in their midst. They always distanced themselves from him. One day his brothers threw him in a pit and lied to his father that he had been eaten by wild animals.

Later they removed him and sold him as a slave to the Egyptians. In respective of his situation and the challenges he faced in his life. He did not stop to dream. After he refused to commit fornication with his master wife when his master's wife seduced him, he was falsely accused and found himself in prison for thirteen-years. In prison, in regardless of his state, he used his gift to interpret others people's dreams and he did not stop dreaming while he continued to manifest his potential in prison.

One day the king had a dream that even his magician and wise man could not interpret. One of the men Joseph had helped interpret a dream remembered him and he was the only one who would be able interpret it and suitable to solve the problem that the dream meant. Finally, his gift made a way for him into the palace. He became the premier of Egypt.

The Determined Are Not Impulsive

They are patient, willing to wait for their opportunity to bounce. In today's society, we all want everything now. We look for instant success, instant riches and instant gratification. The determined are completely different. They are prepared to wait until their turn shows up.

The Power Of Determination

Sometimes what you want may not be possible now and there may be nothing you can do about it. That is fine. Just be patient while taking a step of accomplishing that thing for the determined can out wait their competition and their adversary. Remember, good things come to those who wait.

The Determined Do Not Let False, Limiting Beliefs Stop Them From Moving Forward.

Determined people do not self-sabotage. Their attitude is that they will find a way through regardless of what might be standing on their way. The saying that, "we are to sleep eight hours a day", don't believe it. It is just a way to limit us from spending much of our twenty-four hours doing more activities that will bring about expansion in our progress. Ask the people who are successful in life and they will tell you. They always go the extra mile. While you are sleeping, they sacrifice some of their sleeping time and have time to work towards their objective to bring additional success.

People can promote false beliefs about things about which they have no experience or proof that they cannot prove. They will tell you cannot do this or that and give you thousands of reasons of why not. Perhaps you can be the first to prove them wrong.

Do not let what you cannot do or what you think you are incapable of stop you from achieving what you want. Les Brown says, "To achieve something you never achieved before, you must be someone you've never been before". Zig Ziglar says, "If you always do what you've always done, you are going to always get what you have always gotten. Far too many people have no idea of what they can do because all they have being told is what they can't do. They don't know what they want because they don't know what's available for them".

The Power Of Determination

The Determined Don't Require the Approval of Others

They do not care what other people think about them, they care only about what they want to achieve and think only about the attainment to achieve their objectives. Their constant self-esteem allows taking bigger challenges. Therefore, as a determined person be sure to listen to your instinct. If it says go while others says do not, do not listen to them as long as you know what you're doing and where your destination lies. As Will Smith says, "Don't listen to the little". Learn to trust your instincts, for determination is based on what you want to do. The importance of the activity you want to do will determine how determined you will be.

Determined People Are Not Lazy.

You cannot reach a R10,000,000 dream if you are still doing a R10 per hour work. If you want to achieve your dreams, you have to out-work, out-hustle and out-think the competition. It is not the extra hours that bring success, but it's what you do with the extra time that matters. Ensure you are taking the right path towards achieving your dreams, otherwise the extra hours will not matter. Work hard and be smart as well. It can be a long ride to the top and you must be willing to pay the price, to do whatever that it takes for as long as it takes, that is, if you want to be at the top. That is what determination is all about.

How to Keep Yourself Going

We have mentioned the things that determined people do not do. Let us consider how to keep going or moving forward as a determined person.

1. Let your past inform you of your future and nothing more.
2. See your life and future as totally within your control.
3. Learn to ignore the things that you cannot control or that you cannot change.
4. Don't be jealous.
5. Don't let complaints, critics and whining stop you.

The Power Of Determination

6. Do not try to impress others or focus on others, rather try to impress yourself.
7. Count your blessings.

Let Your Past Inform You of Your Future and Nothing More.

The past is important. Learn from your mistakes. Learn from others' mistakes. Then let it go. It depends on your perspective. When something bad happens to you, see it as an opportunity to be kind, to forgive and learn by understanding that it can happen to you if you are not cautious.

The past is just training and it does not define you. Think about what went wrong but only in terms of how you will make sure that next time you and the people around you will know how to make sure it goes right.

See your Life and Future as Totally Within your Control.

There is a saying that, "pray as if God will take care of all, act as if all is up to you.-(Cool quotes). The same premise applies to luck. Many people feel luck has a lot to do with success or failure. If they succeed, luck favored them. If they failed, luck was against them. Most successful people do feel that good luck played a role in their success. However, they do not wait for good luck or bad luck.

They act as if success or failure is totally within their control. That is a choice with determination. If they fail, they caused it and if they succeeded, they caused it. Instead of wasting your mental energy upon worrying about what might happen to you, you can put all your effort into making the thing happen (And if you get lucky, hey you are even better off.) You cannot control luck, but you can definitely control yourself.

Learn to Ignore the Things that you Cannot Control or that you Cannot Change.

Learn to ignore the things that you cannot have control over. Why waste your time and power on things you cannot control. If you

The Power Of Determination

keep worrying about things that you cannot change, you will waste the time to look for what you can do to bring a change.

For some people family issues and relationships can be controlled. For others politics or global warming are issues that matter. Whatever it is you care about, you may not make others care about. They will not. Rather be determined to bring a change.

Do not be Jealous

When a friend does something awesome, that does not prevent you from doing something awesome or even better. As a matter of fact, where success is, birds of a feather tend to flock together. So draw your successful friend even closer. Do not be jealous, just create and celebrate awesomeness wherever you find it. In time, you'll find more of it in yourself.

Don't Let Complaints, Critics and Whining Stop you

Your words have power especially over you. Whining about your problem always makes you feel worse, not better. So if something is worrying you, don't waste time complaining, but put that mental energy into making the situation better (unless you want whine forever, eventually you'll have to make it better).

So why waste time? Fix it now. Do not talk about what is wrong. Talk about how you will make things better, even if that conversation is with yourself only. Do the same with your friend. Do not just be a shoulder to your friend. Friends do not let friends whine; friends help friends make life better. Friends help friends to breakthrough to the other side.

Do Not Try to Impress Others or Focus on Others; Rather Try to Impress Yourself

Are you yourself or somebody else? Are you living for yourself or for others? Not everyone likes your clothes, your title, your possessions and your accomplishments. Those are all things. People can be in your company even smile at you, but it does not mean that they like you. As you know, people pretend a lot and the heart of many is ungrateful and envious.

Surely many may seem to like you, but within they are opposite. A relationship based on substance is not a genuine relationship. A genuine relationship will be found when you stop trying to impress others, and start trying to be yourself. Spend time with people who really matter in your life. If you are going to live your life to satisfy the pleasures of others, you will live under pressure and you will not be yourself and will not be fulfilling your actual dreams. Remember what brings greatness is being yourself.

Count your Blessings
Before you turn off the light every night, take a moment to stop worrying about what you do not have. Think about what you have. You have a lot to be thankful for. Feel good about yourself. Feeling better about yourself is the best way of all to recharge your mental energy and will power to determination.

Therefore, as you walk towards fulfilling your goals remember to be disciplined.

Discipline
Discipline is the ability to do something continually. Do not eat too much, instead sacrifice. When your stomach is too full your brain works slowly. Remember that honey is good but if you eat too much of it, you will vomit. If you are disciplined enough, anything that will not allow you to fulfill your destiny will separate you from your goals. Most unsuccessful people today lack discipline; and lack of discipline is what makes many people create excuses for their lack of success in life.

Commit your Plans to God
Remember also to commit your plan to God so that he will make them successful and that he may direct your path. Remember it is

The Power Of Determination

God who knows the exact plans or path that will give you the kind of a future that you are hoping for.

'For I know the plans that I have for you,' declares the LORD, 'plans for welfare and not for calamity to give you a future and a hope.' *Jeremiah29:11.* (NASB)

Be serious

This world is not designed to give you anything for free. Anything that is for free somebody has paid for it. The world will never give you what you want. You must create what you want. You're the one who has to work for what you want. You must go for it. Every one of us is born with a form of greatness within.

Your greatness is within. It will never manifest unless you unleash it. You are the one that has to active it. Remember also not to leave faith behind. Anything you want to do, don't wait to see it before you do it. Take a step forward and you will see that it will work out for you. For we work not by sight, but by faith.

For you shall be saved by your own faith. We walk not by sight, but by faith with hope and patience that never fails. Anytime you look back, you will not see greatness. Disappoint your disappointment and do not be afraid to take risk. For all the great men before man and all the great men before God are all the product of risks. This is the power of determination.

The Power Of Determination

Poems

The Power Of Determination

Who's At Fault?

The day she drew my attention
It was sweet as honey.
I pierced what was in my chest.
The girl accepted my petition.
Our forefathers did not lie when they said:
Even if you walk in a valley your head will be visible.

While I never thought of it.
She told me that I have broken her leg. I started crashing my head. Like
a heavy rock it was.
I never ate the bones of the head as on this day.
Another day in the morning,
While the sun was placing its nose upon the earth
My mother knocked my room door. I came out.
I found two woman followed by my flower.
My heart set itself upon my throat. I was falling short of air. Felt like the
earth could open and swallow me.
It was twice sundown for me.

When I sat down, I saw my father coming.
That's when the two women pierced the potatoes.
I saw my father falling from the chair.
He started flowering tears of an infant.
The rain fell upon him without clouds.

At end he lifted up his mouth stated:
They are both my children"
They are both of my blood.
The water has been poured on the soil already.

The Power Of Determination

Donkey

You're humble.
You're obedient.
You do not make noise.
You do not announce yourself.

You're controllable unlike the wild-calf.
The king chose to ride you instead of the horses.
Whatever direction you're ordered to follow,
You follow.

You allow yourself to carry heavy load,
Heavy duties.
You do not complain much.
You survive hardships in the wilderness.
You do not murmur much.

Above the camels and horses, the son of man prefers you for even the
son of God chose to ride on you.

The Power Of Determination

Education

You're the source of knowledge.
Your first born is wisdom.
Your granddaughters and sons are development.
For you replace an empty mind with an open one.

The Power Of Determination

Jesus

You're life
You're redeeming
A sign of respect
A sign of appreciation.

You're a source of strength.
You give strength to the weak,
Provide courage to the weary.
You mend broken hearts.

You strengthen our mortal bodies,
Heal our pain,
And give hope to the hopeless.
You heal our sickness and diseases.

You place a smile on the faces of the poor.
You're the bread of life.
More powerful than any double-edged sword,
You're the source of strength to mankind.
You're the word of God the creator.

The Power Of Determination

Farmers

You're producers.
You're planters, not eaters.
You create duties.
You prefer to employ instead of being an employee.

You can predict the future.
You plan and work
You do not chase what is not yours;
You see riches in the wilderness.

You're stable and able.
You're creative.
You're content with what you have.
You do not lose a seed due to a strange appetite.

You're a giver, a producer and a lender.
You see the treasures of life in the hidden.
You're an investor.
You're the source of supply to the souls of mankind.

The Power Of Determination

Anger

You're cruel.
You're an enemy to joy.
You're an enemy of peace.
You're an enemy of happiness.

When you appear our smiles fade away.
Where you appear things fall apart.
You're a seed of wounds and hurts.
You're opposite to unity.

You're the source of bitterness.
Envy is your grandmother.
You're a king to the short-tempered.
The short-temped are your slaves.

The Power Of Determination

Life

When life knocked me down,
I was like a seed buried, forgotten and rejected,
Alone and lonely in the shadow of life,
Bored and meditating,

Seeking for a solution, but nothing came to mind.
Destiny helpers dispersed.
All hope was gone and I had faith in nothing.
All courage was gone like a mist.

I found no rest for the brain.
All my thoughts-soldiers were working day and night,
Just eating the bones of the head.
My peace of mind was shuttered away.

All day, all night my soul, troubled by the battles of life,
Was longing and striving for the better life in the hidden.

The Power Of Determination

Death

When you're in your abode
People forget about your existence,
But the day you strike!
Tears are set on fire.

Afflicting us as painful as the snake venom,
When you invade, all the joy fades away!
Go there - Go there - service - service.

Don't think we're talking to the creator here.
It is your presence that is honored.
In your invasion you don't knock.
You hit with stick and take the one your heart is longing for,
Bringing sorrow and grief to families and their relatives.

On the sunrise and sundown you visit anywhere you want,
But you were never invited.
If you could give a sign, we would run away from you.

When we begged for your pardon, you jumped and licked the sky.
Do you have a relationship with Satan?
Or are you sent by the creator?
When the sun sets its nose upon the earth, you hear them saying:
That night you have stolen a clay pot.
You'll hear them saying:
The jacket is full of char.
You'll hear them saying:
The snail has collected ashes.
You'll hear them saying:

The black cloud has fallen upon us.

In other places you have agitated their heart.
How strong are your teeth?
Who do you exercise with?

The Power Of Determination

Your power is so astonishing;
You cannot even be jailed.

For you are unstoppable; for to run away from you is to give ourselves
into your hands.
If you could sing, you would get flying colors every time.
You're even a song of the frogs among mankind.

The Power Of Determination

The Norm of These Days

Where are the lifestyles of the olden days?
The ancient days were better than nowadays.
The children had respect for the law.
Respect was their belt.

But has all gone with the past?
You give them principle;
Old fashioned and barbaric it is, they say.
We are a new generation.

The children have become the mothers and the fathers.
A child gives birth to a child.
The father is terrified by his son,
The daughter is competing with her mother.

The teacher is afraid of the learner.
The spirit of teaching and learning is fading away.
The law of nature is changing.
The children are now fighting the rod.

Things are falling apart.
The shepherd is chased by the sheep.
The child is no longer afraid to raise her mouth.
She is feeding her parents with broken bottles.

What has fallen upon us, oh mankind?
We must seek salvation or we shall all be led to our doom.

The Power Of Determination

My Appointed Time

Like the wind blowing the straw
Back and fro
So you rule our lives.
We all depend on you like worms of soil that depends upon the wet soil
for survival.
Your ruler ship is like a cedar in Lebanon.
With patience I wait for you, like a farmer who awaits the harvest.

But it's just as always.
You keep me waiting.
I long for the future
Like a bride who waits for the bridegroom who has gone to war so I am.

I do not lose my patience.
My hopes do not fade away.
I long to be upon my throne of greatness.
When is my appointed time?

The Power Of Determination

Who am I?

I found myself in a circular shape
Called planet Earth.
I was formed in a womb.
I was just from a nine-month battle.
I came out as a little giant.
I kept growing every day and
Things kept changing every day.
I found myself again in planet,
The world of Imagination
I started eating the bones of the head.

Asking myself who am I?
Where do I belong?
What's the purpose of my existence?
What are my direction, vision and mission in life?
Where is my compass navigating to?

An answer came.
You're an agent of change it said,
But I didn't understand.
I continued asking myself what was an agent of change?
There I was, given a manual of my life
Stating you're a child of destiny
Destined for greatness.
I was born to shine my light.
I am the light of the world.
That cannot be comprehended by natural mind.
I am the clone of the Creator.

The Power Of Determination

Inexorable Time

Time I'm calling you.
Can you answer my call?
Can you be available to answer my questions?
Will you grant me my request?
I tried to stop you, but you refused.
I'm always left behind because of you.
Where do you come from?
I hear you existed from the very beginning,
Some say you're the king of ages.
You rule our lives.
You carry authority.

Many have tried to stop you; you refused.
You're always busy and forward. You never stop.
Don't you get tired?
Tell me the secret behind your deeds.

I look around. Many are crying because of you.
You left them behind. Why?
Some say you didn't allow them.
Why is everyone afraid of you?
Why even take full respect even from the elders?
I see you reigning every day.
Who placed you in power?
Why did you take their choices?
Who gave you authority?
Anyone who rebels against you is led to destruction.
Why is it so? Tell me. I want to know.
I am the clone of the Creator.
Who are you?

The Power Of Determination

Mentees

Are you their sheep?
Are they not your leaders?
Have they not given themselves unto thee?
Like a shepherd who gives his life for his sheep.
Why do you rebel against them?
Why criticise them after all?
Have they not shown you enough love and kindness?
They gave themselves to you; they found you like sheep without a
shepherd, took care of you.

They made you. You're because they were.
But you tore it all apart. You now manifest a seed that they did not plant
in you.
You have forgotten all their good deeds towards you.
They mentored you.
They raised you into greatness.
They gave you a site of greatness.

But now your chest resists them with immediate effect.
Why have thou abandoned them and forgotten.
Why do you despise their command?
Why leave behind principles of life?
Is it not they who raised you?
Placed you into power?
But you have turned them into failure.
Fallen heroes you have made them.
Like someone who is living dead
You have buried them alive, why?
Do not forget that whatsoever a man sows, so shall he reap.

The Power Of Determination

My Creator

I am yours, your majesty.
I am yours, oh my heavenly father.
I come across thorns that are traps,
Without my intentions they trap me.
But I never forget you.

Your name has roots in my heart.
I fall into temptations without cline
I find myself swimming in sin.
It's not my wish, father.
It's just a disease in my blood.
Deliver me from temptation and situations that sap my strength.
I find myself in bad deeds.

But this is not my will, oh father.
It's Satan who is jealous.
Pride has kept me silent.
Have mercy on me, oh Jehovah,
For I am your beloved one.

The Power Of Determination

My Destiny Is Everyone's Guess

I am who I am.
I come from whence I came.
Sure of my destination,
But unsure of when I will arrive.
My destiny,
My future,
My tomorrow,
When will I be with you?
When will I catch up with you?
Will my dreams not fade away like the mist?
Yes, it's all up to me,
For I am my own master.
I am the driver of my own faith.
In the middle of the ocean,
Still swimming upon the waves,
To the other side I will arrive.

The Power Of Determination

My Children

My children,
You're my offspring.
Today you're happy that you're fed and satisfied.
All that you need is at the table. Today you do show off.
Don't forget that the cloth you wear and all you're having we just
bought for you.

Don't forget that you are growing up.
Don't forget that there is tomorrow.
Don't forget that you are not chickens,
You are eagles.
But we, your parents, won't be there for you tomorrow.
Are you going be able to feed yourself?
Are you brave enough to survive in the jungle of life?
For it takes a predator to survive in the jungle.

Do you ever think about your tomorrow?
Do you ever think about where you come from and where you're going?
Do you know who you are?

My children, we are just passing by.
As for you, the journey is still long.
What are you planning for your tomorrow?
Here is earth. You must sweat for anything you want.
Do not seek what is not yours,
For what is not yours will be taken away from you.
Don't strengthen yourself with what you'll inherit.
For it shall be eaten by termites.
It is not yours.
Yours is to walk your own journey.

Remember one word is enough for the wise.
Do not curse us when we are upon our graves,
For we have bitten your ears.
But a fool will never take heed. I charge you that don't be so.

The Power Of Determination

Don't live among the chickens.
Don't forget who you are.
You are eagles,
My children.

The Power Of Determination

My Mother

You're a mother indeed.
Your heart is filled with kindness and love.
You allowed a battle in your womb due to my creation
For my safety.
Out of you came a hero.
You did not abort away my destiny.
The Creator entrusted you as my transportation to this earth.

Many claim to be mothers, yet they are murderers.
They have murdered destinies.
You're a mother indeed.
I am because you are.
You let me hide in your womb 'til I was prepared to break forth, to
manifestation.
I salute your mother Majesty
Long life unto you, mother.

The Power Of Determination

How Long Must I Train?

I was born yesterday.
I hear that I have to be made.
I have been in many hands
I have climbed many mountains and hills.
It's not experience that I have,
But it's just like that.

How long must I wait?
When will I be put into greatness?
When will I be considered?
Must I wait for Christ's arrival?

I have being waiting.
Is not wisdom and knowledge enough?
Am I not wise as a serpent?
Have I not served enough?
When is my promotion?

When will I be in power?
How long must I wait?
I have waited so long.
My patience is fading away.

Are not the youth the strength of the nation?
Yet I am not considered.
Must I give up?
When is my time of greatness?

The Power Of Determination

Leaders

Should not a leader lead by example?
Why have you led us astray?
We obeyed you, trusted you.
We gave you respect to the fullest.
You were our role model.

You let us down.
Your own words are now condemning you.
You brought destruction, and destruction has fallen upon you.
Why have you violated the nations?
We were your sheep.
Must we be like you?
We are now like flocks without a shepherd.
What type of a leader are you?
For you do not practise what you preach.
Your own deeds are mocking you.

We thought you were our best.
Your realities are not real.
You're a myth.
We'd rather be like ants without a king than to be led astray.
Where are you leading us?

The Power Of Determination

Destiny

Why is it that destiny takes away the people we love?
Why is it that we always face trouble because of our destiny?
We come across thorns of life that prick us without cline.
They prick us in spite of our intentions.

Why do we face difficulty before fulfilling our destiny?
Many couldn't reach their destiny. Why?
Many tried to go beyond their destiny, but they failed. Why?
Without recognition of their destiny, people perish.
Anyone who does not consider his destiny becomes lost.
Without destiny there is no direction.
Your destiny has always been there and will always be.
For our destiny is the reason why we were born.

The Power Of Determination

Ungrateful People

Ungrateful people,
Why are you selfish?
Why are you stingy and greedy?

You don't care about other people.
You don't care about other people's feelings.
You don't care whether others are hurt or not.
Your character and attitude are harmful.

Many spent their money and time to aid you.
Many sacrificed at the expense of their families to help you.
Now that you've been made great, you're ungrateful.
Why don't you pay respect of appreciation to your coaches, mentors
and teachers?

All you are is a proud look.
You are selfish and greedy.
You manifest foolishness.
Is that how you show your appreciation?
Why be ungrateful?

The Power Of Determination

The Critics

What has he done?
Is he not innocent?
Is he not obedient and humble?
After all he has done for you; you don't appreciate and respect him.

You make false speeches against him.
You are rebellious and stubborn.
I try to forget you, but your character always displays itself.
Why don't you just live?
Why poison the well that you have drunk from?
Why do you want to ruin his well?
Where will the others drink from?
You're violating him.
Will good deeds be repaid by evil?
Surely your end shall come
For the mouth that mocks him today will congratulate him tomorrow.

I know who he is.
May you live to see his success.

The Power Of Determination

Sugar Daddies

Sugar Daddies, what are you?
Are you not murderers of destinies?
You have destroyed many destinies and lives of so many young girls.
You deceived them with your evil offer of gifts in return for sex.
Do you imagine what you're doing to the daughter of man?
Imagine another man, a married man, sleeping with your own daughter.
Are you kind?
Do you have the gift of love within you?
How does it feel to see your own daughter sleeping with another
married man like you?
Do you care about her life?
Do you care about the future of our nation?
If yes; why are you destroying the lives of our young ladies?
If you have enough money, why not sponsor them to do things that will
benefit their lives in a positive way?
Why are you destroying the life and destiny of a young lady?
Her destiny was aborted by you.
She was destined to come and bring a solution to us, but you aborted
her away.
Are you not a murderer, a destroyer and deceiver?
You're a murderer of destiny.
What are you doing to the young ladies?
Would you want another sugar daddy to do the same to your daughter?
Why not your daughters?
Then, why do it to the daughter of man?
For the Creator is angry with you.
You're violating his creatures?
Your reward will surely arrive.
Destruction awaits you.

The Power Of Determination

Sugar Mommies

What type of a mommy are you?
You're like a slow poison.
You're a sugar murderer.
What have you chosen to become?
Are you the destroyer of young men's destinies?
Are you a mother?
Do you have a son?
Do you know the cost and pain of giving birth to a child?
No. Don't know, right?
You have set yourself on the mission of destroying the destiny of another woman's son.
Do you know what that young man could have become if he hadn't fallen into your arms?
You trap the young men and you let them taste the wrath of your fornication.
You're destroying families.
You're destroying the future husband of another young lady somewhere.
You're destroying the heads of our nation.
You let them taste the wrath of your fornication and adultery.
You lead the young men to destruction.
You know man is the head.
You refuse to lead them in the right path.
You choose to destroy the soul of young men by letting them taste the wrath of your fornication and adultery.
Are you married?
Would you prefer your husband to be a sugar daddy?
Do you have a son?
Do you wish your son to have a sugar mummy?
If you were a normal person filled with love and kindness, would you feel better if your son was under the trap of another sugar mummy like you?
Do you have a daughter?

The Power Of Determination

How would it be to you, being a mother, having another man (a sugar daddy) destroying the destiny of your daughter, her future, leading her to activities that lead to death and destruction?
Sugar Mommies, you're destroying the future of our young men.
Your gifts are for a moment.
They lead to death and destruction.
Stop violating the principles of nature.
You're destroying the law of respect and dignity.
The Creator is angry with you.
If you do not repent; watch out for destruction, for it awaits you.

The Power Of Determination

The Youth

What are you waiting for?
You have stayed long.
Your mates have left you.
You have stayed in the shadow long enough.
Weeks, months and years have passed by.
Why do you sit upon your hands?
Don't you know to sit upon your hands produces poverty?

Go out. It's enough. For you are left behind.
You will not be a youth forever.
Go out and work.
Create the future you hope for.
Build the future.
You are our future tomorrow.
What type of tribes and generations do you hope for?
Some dream, yet others wake up and work.
What do you do?
Laziness produces poverty.
It is the hand of the diligent that shall rule.
Accept advice and reminders before days will be gone and you will have no pleasure in them.
For it is foolishness to hate advice.
Be wise and you will rule the affairs of men.
Arise for your journey is too long.

The Power Of Determination

People With and Without a Purpose

I walk upon the road of life trying to explore the world.
I see people going up and down, people with and without purpose,
people with direction and people without direction.

I see people pursuing their desires that are not pursuable, people
walking in corruption trying to be satisfied, but they are never filled.
I see people trying to make life better, but to them it's just like here.

I see people with different companies, the good and the bad, with the
good corrupting the bad, the bad ruining the good.
I see people going up and down, looking for nothing, for nothing.
I see mothers leaving their families to explore life, fathers leaving their
home like birds that leave their nest.
I see some people experiencing failure, but never concerned about
success; others not concerned about tomorrow.
I see people trading and bartering on the process, ladies selling their
gold for money, unconcerned about the consequences.
I see robbers of destiny on their mission, people never content with
what they have and achieved, men never satisfied.
Oh mankind. What is your purpose?
What is your choice?
What is your tomorrow?
You have been sleeping too long.
Don't you know that to sit upon your hands will bring poverty?
What is your direction?
What type of a future are you creating for yourself?
Arise!
Time has left you.
You're left behind.
Your mate has left you.

The Power Of Determination

Shade your Future

Your future, your choice,
Your tomorrow, your action,
Your actions, your intentions,
Your intentions, your choices.

An Artist you are.
It's all in your hand.
Draw it up.
Make it all happen.

Paint your future.
Make a picture of your tomorrow.
Don't only imagine it,
Make the image reality.

Draw a picture.
Let us see it.
Shade your destiny.

The Power Of Determination

My Destiny

I am a child of destiny.
I was born to be a leader, a shepherd.
I was born a nation.
I am a child of destiny, an agent of change.
The nations have being waiting for me.
I am not a biological mistake.
I am not the product of a man and a woman who cannot hold their sexual feelings.
I am not a coincidence.
I am a child of destiny, not a destitute.

I was planned by the Creator.
My life has existed in the mind of the Creator.
I am the plan of God.
I have been created and manufactured by God.
I will fulfil my destiny.
Regardless of what happens, I will fulfil my destiny, for my destiny is in the hand of God.
My condition is not my conclusion.
I know my pains will pay a gain.
My today is not my tomorrow.
My destiny is my choice,
My future tomorrow.

The Power Of Determination

The Ungrateful Generation

How long will you be ungrateful?
How long will you be self-centred?
Why is it that you don't care about other people?
You're disrespectful and ungrateful.
I did not plant this seed in you.

Why do you urinate in the well you drink from?
Why pollute the stream you drink from?
Will you not need it one day?
Where do you want others to drink from?
You were found like sheep without a shepherd, lost and rejected.
I mothered you.
I made you what you are.
I invested in you, but you led me into a great loss; you profited me not.
Now that you're made, you march in rebellion. Your chest resists my authority.
You were humble.
Now that you're exalted, you take no heed.
How long will you be ungrateful?
Can you point your father's house with a finger? Can good be repaid with evil?

Surely you repaid me with bitterness.
How long will you be foolish?
I remind you.
Never forget that reality will always be real.
A man shall reap what he sows.
The beginning has an end.
Why have you forgotten all they have done for you?
People spent their money and their time on you.
Is that how you repay them?
They sacrificed their families and pleasures to attend to you.
But today you repay them with ungratefulness.
Do not be deceived.
We put you up and down you shall come.

The Power Of Determination

It is a taboo that a ruler shall rule forever.

You're led to your own destruction.
Surely God is not mocked.
You shall reap what you have sown, you ungrateful generation.

The Power Of Determination

Blank Mind

You lack wisdom and understanding.
You're blank and damp.
Your head is filled with water.
You despise wisdom.
Why refuse to turn your eyes unto understanding?
Why refuse to learn what is good?

Have you forgotten that wisdom is the principal talent?
Make wisdom your sister.
Make understanding your special friend.
Make knowledge your daily bread.

Take teachings instead of pleasures that will fade away like the mist.
You'll find much learning to be of use,
For by wisdom, kings rule and make their laws fair.
Ask Solomon the wise king.
He'll tell you wisdom calls for you.

The Power Of Determination

The Strange Woman

Her lips are sweet as honey.
Her talk is smooth as cool music that relaxes the mind.
Her feet go after the pleasures of the like.
She's unlovable, but they all fall for her.
Her way leads to death and destruction.
Her fountain flows and satisfies, but it's all filled with poisons.
She has taught many to taste the wrath of her fornication and adultery.
Her beauty shines like a smiling strawberry.
Don't fall into her traps.

Her heart wants to fool and trap someone.
She is attractive like the flowers hunted by bees to form honey,
But she feeds with poison.
She'll satisfy her hunger and thirst and leave you with death and
destruction.

Her feet do not stay at home.
She has no other mission, but to steal, to kill and to destroy.
She knows her master very well.
Without mercy her master is and without mercy she is.
The strange woman she is.

The Power Of Determination

Nature of Africa

My Africa,
Africa my continent,
The inheritance of our forefathers.
Where are you?

Where are the colors of your beauty?
Where are your garments?
Where is your image, Africa?
Am talking about your identity.

Are they all taking it from you?
They have taken your treasures.
But let not your culture fade away from you.
What about your melodies?

Where's the real you, Africa?
Are you still Africa?
What proof do you have?
Where are the poems praising Africa?

What about your incantations and chants?
Where's the African food?
The African recipes?
Where's your dignity, Africa?
Where's your pride?

Where are your forests and valleys with the birds of peace that sing
your songs?

Where's the forest for the hunter?
What about a fertile plot for the farmer?
Can't you see your ways of life?
Your image and your reality are fading away with the ages?

You taught your children laws of respect.

The Power Of Determination

I mean a generation of respect, love, peace and happiness.
A generation with fear for the elders
It's all fading away.
Where are you, Africa?

The Power Of Determination

The Beauty of the Nature of Africa

There is nothing more to my Africa than
The wild flowers that breathe the innocent breath,
Animals that live freely,

The beauty of the sunset,
The beauty of the sunrise and sundown,
The mountains that are steep and brilliantly formed.

The birds that sing in the east to the west,
The leopard that runs to the west,
The droplets that pour on our roof,
The rivers flowing from east to west,
Dividing war and peace.

The stars that shine throughout the night lightening up our face at night,
The beauty of Africa.

The Power Of Determination

The Woman of Africa: The Ebony Beauty

Our African queens
Our African princesses
Your color, your pride
Your color, your inheritance.

Am speaking about the color of your skin.
Am speaking about your color.
Your black color I mean,
Your brown color I mean.
Your multi-color I mean.
Am speaking about your ebony beauty.

The pride of a black woman
That suit the flowers of your culture,
The garment of your traditions,
The pride of Africa.

The image that the creator has adorned you with.
Your strength and ability,
Your gift of multi-tasking,
Let it not fade away from you.

Be proud of who you are.
Do not terminate the colors of your skins.
Do not let your color become extinct.
They suit your African garment.
You're good and wonderful as you are.

Your ebony beauty is the flower of Africa.
Do not change yourself.
Remember who you are,
An African princess,
An African queen.

Let your African ebony beauty shine.

The Power Of Determination

Be judged not by the color of your skin,
But by your character.
For beauty is from within.

The Power Of Determination

Have Farmers' Mentality, not Hunters' Mentality

Why not have hunters' mentalities? Hunters are eaters not planters. Hunters look for what has already being made; but farmers are creators.

Hunters are people with strange appetites. They are never satisfied with whatever they have and they think only about what to eat.

Farmers create jobs while hunters look for jobs to do; they do not have the assurance of what they will catch or kill, but farmers can predict their future and what they will achieve.

Hunters go after what they do not have. When you chase what is not yours, you'll lose what is yours. A hunter does not see far when they are in the wilderness, but a farmer sees beyond a wilderness. When they see wilderness they think of a firm of production (farm).They think of everlasting creation of success.

Hunters are not stable. They move from one forest to the other. They kill only to eat. But farmers are stable and content and consistent with what they have; they predict what must be achieved is as they have planned.

The Power Of Determination

Money

Money separates some people from God their creator. Money makes us to have pride and it locks us into sin and makes some people ungrateful.

You can buy a bed, but you can't buy sleep. You can buy a book and read, but you can't buy wisdom. You can buy a passport to travel to any nation, but you can't buy a passport to heaven.

There are many things that we do with money. A woman can turn to authorise her husband because she has more money than her husband. A person can disrespect his or her parents because he or she has money.

Even the foolish believe that there is no God because of money. You can see a person lifting up green and red leaves before the congregation, so that they can admire him in the church.

A man leaves his family to join companions that lust for the pleasures of the world. Some people also do not honour others because they have money, but when money is not there we tend to be humble.

When money is there, friends will be there, but when money is not there, friends will go. We feel empowered when we have money, but when money is not there we become like straws that can be blown anywhere by the wind.

A person can help to endanger the life of an individual to get money. Even Satan can move a person out of his family to unknown destination because of money. He can recruit a person by that which is not beneficial and tends to make it beneficial and that which leads to death and destruction.

People can lead themselves into the traps of sin and death just to get money. Some children have raged war against their parents because of money. Money has the power to make things fall apart. It invades a relationship and leaves it in pieces.

The Power Of Determination

Money drew many to their grave before their time. Let's all pray to the almighty to help us understand the issue of money.

A husband and his wife in their caves, they shout and insult each other because of money. Children fighting their parent because they need money; which the parent does not have. Money makes us to fight against God. Some rebels who are proud, arrogant and disrespectful are the product of money.

The children of mankind can fill the compound of a person because they have seen money. You can see a wife leaving her children and husband and depart the house by the window in the night to run after a man who has money.

All these are the works of money. A learner can abandon his studies to pursue the lust of the flesh because his parent has money. May the creator have mercy and give us wisdom and the ability to put aside the devil and tell him "Satan take your money for it puts us into trouble and problems" that peace may invade. Some people are foolish because they have money.

We can see nations not relating with other nations that do not have money. Some people unable to live, eat and survive because of money. The children of mankind are fighting each other just because of money. Mankind, let us join hands together and let there be peace, joy and happiness among us.

The Power Of Determination

Glossary

To eat bottles: to be angry.

The fig that is pink. Has a warm inside: a woman who is beautiful in most cases tends have bad character or inner side.

To eat the bones of the head: to think deeply.

To hit each other with a baboon's bones: to quarrel.

To pierce the potato: to reveal a secret or let known something that is or was a secret.

The jacket is full of air: someone has passed away.

The snail has collected ashes: someone has died.

To be covered by a black cloud: someone has died in their family or they are having a funeral.

To stir up or give a wasp: to cause trouble.

To break a leg: to impregnate a young woman illegitimately.

To have a burnt mouth: To speak too much or to use verbal words especially during a quarrel or disagreement.

To cross each other's legs: to quarrel or fight.

To jump and lick the sky: to deny.

The Power Of Determination

Other books by this Author

Destiny is a Matter of Choice

The Power Of Determination

About the Publisher

Mr. William Jenkins was born in Ottawa, Canada in 1932. After completing a degree in Mathematics and Physics at Queen's University at Kingston in 1954, he became a computer programmer and worked in that field for 45 years. Subsequently, he sold residential real estate and then wrote and published a few mystery stories for middle-school children.

He is especially interested in publishing stories and poems from students. A few students from South Africa have submitted their writing.

If you are a teacher or student, submit creative writing as an email attachment to

williamhenryjenkins@gmail.com.

There is no charge for services. The only out of pocket cost to Mr. Jenkins for this hobby is the cost of printing and shipping a few copies of the paperback, one to the Library of Canada, Legal Deposit, others to the authors.

The Power Of Determination

The Power Of Determination

Notes